Everyone l ...
that is, ex ...
the greatest story ever ... ...
of stories—the Bible! Joe Deegan helps us
to rediscover the power of story, why it's so
effective and why we need to rediscover it for
today's world. You'll enjoy this book.

Paul E. Miller
Author of *A Praying Life*
Founder of 'seeJesus' ministries

Story stays with us and can help us see the
truth. *The Power Of Story* goes straight to the
heart with this *Track* series, building a bridge
between God's Word and our lives in real
time. This new series is a winsome resource for
teenagers, helping them to know and believe
that God meets us right where we are.

Sandra McCracken
Singer-songwriter

We all love a good story. *The Power of Story* is
about stories, but not just any story. It's about
the greatest story of all. Teens, read this book
to learn how your story was written to fit into
God's great big story.

Christina Fox
Author of *Tell God How You Feel*

Joe Deegan has reminded us of the power of the greatest story ever told, the gospel story told from Genesis 1 to Revelation 22. It's the story that redeems our past, transforms our present and secures our future with Christ in eternity. This is not a book simply about the power of a story, but rather the power in the gospel story. I am encouraged as I read it, and I hope it encourages you the same.

Robbie Seay
Singer-songwriter

TRACK
CULTURE

A STUDENT'S GUIDE TO
THE POWER
OF STORY

JOE
DEEGAN
SERIES EDITED BY
JOHN PERRITT

CHRISTIAN
FOCUS

tym

Copyright © Joe Deegan 2021

paperback ISBN 978-1-5271-0695-6
ebook ISBN 978-1-5271-0782-3

10 9 8 7 6 5 4 3 2 1

First published in 2021
by
Christian Focus Publications Ltd,
Geanies House, Fearn, Ross-shire,
IV20 1TW, Great Britain

www.christianfocus.com

with

Reformed Youth Ministries,
1445 Rio Road East
Suite 201D
Charlottesville,
Virginia, 22911

Cover by MOOSE77

Printed by Page Bros, Norwich

CONTENTS

Series Introduction

Christianity is a religion of words, because our God is a God of words. He created through words, calls Himself the Living Word, and wrote a book (filled with words) to communicate to His children. In light of this, pastors and parents should take great efforts to train the next generation to be readers. *Track* is a series designed to do exactly that.

Written for students, the *Track* series addresses a host of topics in three primary areas: Doctrine, Culture, and the Christian Life. *Track's* booklets are theologically rich, yet accessible. They seek to engage and challenge the student without dumbing things down.

One definition of a track reads: *a way that has been formed by someone else's footsteps.* The goal of the *Track* series is to point us to that 'someone else'—Jesus Christ. The One who forged a track to guide His followers. While we cannot follow this track perfectly, by His grace and Spirit He calls us to strive to stay on the path. It is our prayer that this series of books would help guide Christ's Church until He returns.

In His Service,

John Perritt
RYM's Director of Resources
Series Editor

1. Stories Shape Us

Nothing keeps a child in line like a good old-fashioned list of rules...said no one *ever*. For most kids, rules are simply windows into new and exciting possibilities. I never noticed how soft and appealing my neighbor's lawn was until he put up the 'keep off the grass' sign. I was never more hungry or thirsty than when I walked into a room with a sign that read, 'no food or drinks allowed.' Rules tend to have the opposite of the intended effect, and believe it or not, adults have been wise to this act for years now. So how is it that they get kids to listen to them?

Well, around the fifteenth century in Europe, a new parenting trend began sweeping across the land. Most people back then lived in small towns, villages, and farming communities surrounded by woods and wildlife. These communities were typically led by parents who wanted to see their children grow up to be healthy, God-fearing adults who knew the difference between right and wrong.

But the adults knew that if you tell a kid not to be disrespectful, they'll stick their tongue out as soon as you turn away. You tell a kid not to be lazy, and they'll do everything in their power to keep from working. You tell a kid not to go into the woods where all the dangerous and interesting animals and vagabonds live, and they'll flock like flies to bug zappers.

So the parents in these communities took a different approach: they traded-in rules for *stories*. As dusk would settle over the villages at nightfall, parents would gather their children around the fire and dazzle them with tales of the forest. They told stories of fairies and princesses and magic and spells and monsters and dragons and little girls and boys who didn't heed their parents' warnings and got swallowed up by witches and wolves when they wandered into the woods. These stories were used instead of rules in order to teach values (be honest, be kind, don't steal, don't lie), and to warn children of the dangers of straying from these principles.

As the children grew older, they passed down the same stories to their own kids. Generation after generation in Europe continued the tradition of telling these same fairy tales to the little ones until one day in the early 1800s, two brothers from Germany named Jakob and Wilhelm Grimm decided to write down a collection of these stories in a book. The title: *Grimm's Fairy Tales.* To this day, they are some of the most famous stories on the planet. Many of us grew up with the Disney versions of these in our very own living rooms—*Snow White and the Seven Dwarves, Cinderella, Sleeping Beauty, Rapunzel, Beauty and the Beast, Little Red Riding Hood,* and *Hansel and Gretel* just to name a few. These are the stories that have been influencing the childhoods of people around the world for over half a millennium now.

And just as parents used stories to shape and mold their children, we see our God doing the same thing throughout Scripture. Now, I know what you're thinking—what about the Ten Commandments? Aren't these just God's big list of rules that He handed down to us from on high? Yes, that's absolutely what they are. But if we're only paying attention to the rules, we're going to miss the story that's wrapped around it.

The Ten Commandments are part of a greater narrative. The Bible is a story that shows us over and over again what it looks like when the commandments are broken and what it looks like when they are kept. And there's only One Person who has kept the commandments perfectly, and He just so happens to be the Hero of this story—but we're getting ahead of ourselves.

GOD GAVE US A LOVE FOR STORIES

Stories shape us in ways that very few things can. People say you are what you eat, and we consume stories all day long. Social media, TV, music, movies, school, news, sports, books, friendships, even our own personal dialogue inside our heads—these are the stories that we munch on day in and day out.

The question is, what are these stories doing to our souls? Are they making us more or less human? In other words, are they shaping us more and more into the creatures God made us to be, or are they driving us further and further away from the light of God's presence? Genesis 1:27 says, '…God created man in his own image, in the image of God he created him; male and female he created them.'

When people see my son standing next to me they say, 'That boy is the *spitting image* of you.' (I'm not quite sure where 'spitting' comes from...maybe that's a Southern thing.) The point is that he not only looks like me, he tends to act like me and think like me and enjoy many of the same things I enjoy. In other words, he shares my DNA.

Being made in the image of the Lord means that we were made to love the things that God loves and hate the things that He hates. If someone said to you, 'Let me teach you a lesson,' you'd most likely tense up and lean away from them. If someone said to you, 'Let me tell a story,' you'd lean forward expectantly with open ears. Where do you think that instinct comes from? Our love for stories comes directly from the One who made us. It's woven into our DNA, just as it was for Jesus Himself, the greatest storyteller who ever lived!

Between the four Gospels of Matthew, Mark, Luke, and John, we have record of Jesus telling over 50 different stories and parables to teach and illustrate the truths of His kingdom to His followers. If Jesus, the Creator of Heaven and earth, believed that storytelling was one of the most effective forms of communicating truth to

His listeners, I think it's safe to say that God put a love for stories in our hearts. And if the King of Kings decided to include human beings at the center of His grand historical narrative told throughout the chronicles of Scripture, then I think it's safe to say that we ourselves *are* stories.

Main Point
Stories shape us more than rules.

Questions for Reflection

- Have you ever thought about why you love stories so much?
- Why do you think stories might be more effective than rules are for teaching us?
- Think about all the movies and shows you watched as a child. What did they teach you about what a hero looks like? What did they teach about what a villain looks like? What did they teach you about humor and fear and adventure and love?
- Have you ever thought about how much your childhood stories have shaped the way you think about life right now?
- Have you ever thought about how much the stories you indulge in now are going to shape who you are as an adult?

2. Your Life Is a Story

What do you look for in a good movie? What are some of your favorite books? Whatever stories you love, they all possess some commonalities. In fact, there are three components that all stories share: Construction, Characters, and Conflict.

Construction means it has structure—a beginning, a middle, and an end. Stories also have characters who form relationships that drive the narrative forward. And finally, they have conflict that reveal problems that need to be fixed.

THE CONSTRUCTION IN OUR STORIES

Think about our lives for a moment. They have structure to them: a beginning (we were born), middle (we live), and end (we eventually die). With this structure, we know that our lives are ultimately driven by a God who is in control of everything that happens to us. We still make choices that shape what we do and who we become, and we live with the consequences of those choices. But ultimately, we know that the Lord is sovereign, and that it is His hand which builds the framework of our existence and lays the foundation of our lives. His hand is the one that constructs the story of our days.

Within the structure of our lives, we also see God as a master craftsman who weaves our stories together with the lives of those around us. Our friends, family, neighbors, teachers, classmates, sometimes even people we don't know—they're all characters in our stories. And if we want to get really metaphysical, we could say that certain places and objects are also characters in our stories.

I'm from a tiny town in Alabama called Tuscumbia. In 2009, I moved to Houston, TX, the fourth largest city in the country. I've grown to love the big city I live in, but every time I drive back down Main Street in Tuscumbia, I feel like I'm visiting an old friend.

My hometown, the streets, the trees, the buildings, the smell—these are all characters in my story. So is my bedroom and my first car and the table at Fuzzy's Pizza where I had my first date with my wife. All of these objects and places hold sentimental value because they're attached to sweet memories of my past.

But not all our memories are sweet, are they? I also remember one night in my junior year of high school, standing in my kitchen gripping the back of the chair in front of me when I found out about a friend who had died unexpectedly. I remember the utter shock that slapped me in the face and the way my stomach lurched into a knot that started climbing up into my throat. I had never felt grief like that before, and I didn't know what to do with it.

Which brings us to the third component— conflict. Conflict is a part of my story; it's a part of everyone's. I had a creative writing teacher in college say, 'If you don't have conflict, you don't have a story.'

THE CONFLICT IN OUR STORIES

Because of sin, our stories now contain conflict. Ever since Adam and Eve fell in the Garden, we now live in the wake of their brokenness, feeling the weight of the curse like a cloud hanging over us. Our brokenness goes to sleep with us every night when we close our eyes and wakes up with us first thing in the morning. Sometimes it feels like we can't escape it.

But our story is also one of redemption for those of us who have placed their faith in Jesus. God promises He will not leave His children in their fallen state. He promises to resolve the conflict and renew what was broken. God ultimately redeems this conflict through the crucifixion of His one and only Son on the cross. He also restores us by sanctifying and growing us through His Spirit, and that growth often occurs in the fellowship of other believers. Your life is a story, but your story is not your own.

James 5:13-16 says, 'Is anyone among you suffering? Let him pray. Is anyone cheerful? Let him sing praise. Is anyone among you sick? Let me call for the elders of the church, and let them pray over him...and if anyone has committed sins, he will be forgiven. Therefore, confess your sins to one another and pray for one another, that you may be healed. The prayer of a righteous person has great power as it is working.'

If I were to sum up this passage, I would put it like this—God wants us to share our stories with one another so that we might be healed. He redeems our conflict by bringing people into our lives to walk through our trials and joys alongside us and help point us to the hope we have in Jesus.

THE RELATIONSHIPS IN OUR STORIES

I have a group of friends who get together once or twice a year to fellowship and encourage one another. We usually dedicate special time to sit in a circle and share our stories—what our lives were like growing up, what our families were like, what we struggled with in the past, what we struggle with now, what we enjoy doing with our time, what makes us happy, what makes us sad. Our unwritten rule is that we don't interrupt or offer advice. We just listen to one another and then pray together as James says. The point of all this is not necessarily to teach each other but to *know* each other.

The Christian life was not meant to be lived alone, and when we share our stories with friends, it's like linking arms with someone in the dark. Ultimately, our friendships here on earth point us to the ultimate friendship we have with Jesus (John 15:15).

Relationships form plot-points in our lives that drive our stories forward and remind us that we are here by design. Our days, as random and repetitive as they might seem at times, are not a coincidence. God has written our stories from before the foundations of the earth, and our relationship with Him is ultimately the plot-point that ties everything together, adding purpose and hope to the lives that we lead.

Main Point

Your life is a story that was crafted by a loving Creator.

Questions for Reflection

- What does it mean that your life is a story?
- Why do the relationships in your story matter so much?
- What are some of the worst conflicts in your personal story right now?
- How can you trace those conflicts back to sin and the Fall back in Genesis 3?

3. Your Story Is Not an Accident

I believe some of the best stories in the world right now have come from a little company called *Pixar*. Okay, it's not that little. But their stories are told for little children all over the world yet somehow manage to end up hitting adults right between the eyes.

Pixar has produced some of the funniest, most heart-warming, compelling narratives I've seen in my lifetime—*Inside Out, Up, Toy Story, Finding Nemo, Onward,* and *the Incredibles,* just to name a few.

Several years ago, Pixar animator Emma Coats shared online her '22 Tips For Storytelling' that she had gathered in her years of working with the company, and they are, quite frankly, a goldmine for any aspiring writer or creator. [1]

1   Koo, Ryan, '22 Tips on the Pixar Storytelling Formula' article from the No Film School website, 2012.

Number five on her list stood out to me: 'Simplify. Focus. Combine characters. Hop over detours. You'll feel like you're losing valuable stuff, but it sets you free.' In other words, every character in your story has to serve a purpose to the plot. If they don't serve a real purpose, combine them with someone else, or get rid of them entirely. The story should be as streamlined as possible. *There should be no wasted characters*!

Now, let me ask a question—if the creators of Pixar understand this rule of storytelling, how much more does the God of all creation understand this about the story that He is crafting? He invented storytelling, for crying out loud! I think He knows what He's doing. To put it plainly, you are not a wasted character in His story.

WRITTEN IN GOD'S BOOK

I praise you, for I am fearfully and wonderfully made. Wonderful are your works; my soul knows it very well. My frame was not hidden from you, when I was being made in secret, intricately woven in the depths of the earth. Your eyes saw my unformed substance; in your book were written, every one of them, the days that were formed for me, when as yet there was none of them (Ps. 139:14-16).

The Psalmist here is saying that God has a book, and in that book, He has written down every single one of our days from before we were even born, before we had even been formed in our mother's womb. When the number of our days was zero, God wrote down our stories before the foundations of the world, and it says so right here in Psalm 139.

Now, I don't say this so that you can walk away feeling better about yourself. I'm not trying to boost your ego or tell you *chin up, you're beautiful just the way you are,* and all that jazz. I'm actually saying this to humble you.

You see, we tend to base our meaning and purpose in life on how we feel during certain moments. If I were to ask a typical teenager how their day went, their first response would usually have something to do with how they felt that day. I'm not trying to say that feelings don't matter. God gave us feelings and emotions; it's important to have high emotional intelligence and understand what our feelings are saying about our circumstances.

But, to be frank, your life is about more than just the way you feel. Your life has meaning outside of your own existence because you were not created for yourself. You were created for the glory of your Maker. Your days have been written down in the annals of the Almighty with His own right hand—your story is *not* an accident. This means that in the midst of your conflict, in the darkest of your days, you can lift your head in faith and know that the story's not over yet.

SHAKESPEARE'S COMEDIES

William Shakespeare, who some consider to be the greatest English writer of all time, wrote plays in three different categories— histories, comedies, and tragedies. Histories were based on true events (like *Henry V*), but comedies and tragedies had a uniquely different qualifying characteristic that was actually quite simple.

Comedies, in the old days, didn't have to be funny. They just had to have one simple, distinguishing factor that set them apart from all other stories—a happy ending (*Midsummer Night's Dream, Taming of the Shrew*). Tragedies, on the other hand, had to end in…well… tragedy (*Romeo and Juliet, Hamlet*). If you were watching one of his plays, you would quickly figure out which type you were watching, and you would know what to expect at the end.

If we were to categorize the stories of our lives into Shakespearean classifications, we'd have to say that our lives are *comedies*. Not because they're hilarious (although sometimes they absolutely are), but because they do not end in suffering and catastrophe. They end in beauty. They end with a smiling face and a hand that wipes every tear of sorrow from our eyes.

Singer/songwriter Sandra McCracken has a song called 'Fool's Gold'. The chorus sings, 'But if it's not okay, then this is not the end. And this is not okay, so I know this is not the end.' When we walk through the moments of life where we know something's not right, when things aren't the way they were meant to be, we can rest assured, according to the promises of God, that this is not the end. Your story is not an accident, and your story's not over yet.

Main Point

God personally made you with a specific purpose for His Kingdom.

Questions for Reflection

- What does Psalm 139:14-16 teach us about how God views our lives?
- If we know that our lives are not an accident, how does that affect the way we view hardship and suffering?
- If we know that the Christian's life will end in beauty and glory and all things being made right, how does that affect the way we view hardship and suffering?

4. God's Word Is a Story

God's Word is much more than an instruction manual. Yes, it teaches us. Yes, it gives us lessons. But if life lessons are the only thing we get out of the Bible, then we're missing perhaps the most important point. I believe that first and foremost, the Bible is meant for intimacy before instruction. Instruction is a byproduct. Let me explain.

When I was younger, I used to hear people in Christian circles talk about listening to God. If you were making bad choices, you must not have been listening to God. If you had a big decision coming up, you needed to quiet all the other voices in your life and listen to God's voice.

At their core, those statements aren't incorrect, but they've always left me confused. I had never heard God's voice, and no one had ever taken the time to explain to me what it sounded like. I thought something was wrong with me. I thought perhaps God didn't like me enough to speak to me, or perhaps I wasn't spiritually enlightened enough to hear Him. I so badly wanted God's voice to rattle my ears the way it had Abraham, Isaac and Jacob, but it never happened. I felt like I wasn't part of the family.

Later in my life I had people explain that God's voice was not an audible sound, but rather, a gut feeling—our conscience guiding us in the right direction. That made more sense to me, but I quickly ran into another problem. The only clear thing my gut had ever steered me toward was food. And for every other major decision in my life, I found that I did not have one voice speaking to me—I had *several*. And they all bounced around in my gut like ping pong balls in a lottery machine. How in the world are you supposed to find God's voice in the midst of all that noise?

When I was in high school, someone finally told me the answer, and I realized it had been staring me in the face my whole life. God speaks to us most clearly through the Bible— that's why it's called God's *Word*.

As I began to read the Scriptures and grow in the Word, I realized that it was not at all what I thought it was. It wasn't a GPS telling me which way to turn. It wasn't a Google search engine made to answer all of my questions. It was a story. It was God's own story, and it was meant to shape and mold me to His very own image.

GOD WANTS TO TELL US HIS STORY

Remember a couple of chapters ago when I mentioned how I periodically got together with a group of friends to fellowship and share our stories? Remember how the goal of those stories was not to teach each other (although we often learned very serious and valuable lessons during our time together)? The goal was to know each other better. The goal was love.

Imagine for a moment that Jesus is sitting down in that circle with you and your friends. Everyone takes their turn in the hot seat, and then all eyes turn to Him. Jesus smiles, clears His throat and says, 'I want to tell you My story, but I want to start at the very beginning. It's going to take a long time to tell this story, and you will learn many lessons. You will be taught many truths, and you will be given much instruction. But most of all and more important than anything else, you will know Me.'

That's the Bible.

It's the story of Jesus, and He hovers over every page whether we see Him there or not. It's all one grand narrative that ties together the thread of Creation, Fall, Redemption, and Restoration, throughout the broken, beautiful history of God's people. It's quite frankly the greatest story that's ever been told, and every other great story in the world finds its roots in the Scriptures.

Main Point

God's Word is a story meant to show us who He is and how much He loves us.

Questions for Reflection

- Do you tend to see the Bible as a story or as a boring list of rules?
- My parents gave me many instructions when I was a child. But they also told me about their lives growing up. If they had only ever given me instruction, they would've been little more than teachers. But when they let me *know* them, they showed me how much they loved me as parents.

What does that say about why God chose to tell us a story instead of just giving us a bunch of rules?

- God told His story not just to teach us but to know us and to help us know Him. How might that truth change the way you read your Bible?

5. Advice For Reading God's Story

How often do you read the Bible? I don't know about you, but that's a question that tends to make me feel a little discouraged. Even if we read consistently, we're typically aware that we've wasted time, in some form or fashion, and we could have read more.

I don't ask that question to guilt-trip you. I'm asking it in order to dig down into the root of why we don't often read. I would be willing to bet that you don't often read the Bible because it's intimidating. It's a big and complex book.

Now, we come to this question—*how* do we read the Scriptures? That's the tricky part, right? The Bible is not an easy book to get into, so I have two pieces of advice for reading God's Word. Number one—ask the right question.

ASK THE RIGHT QUESTION
I used to imagine that the Bible was a teacher giving me instructions, and that if I followed all

the instructions to the tee, I would get an 'A' in God's grade book. Then I learned that nobody gets an 'A' in God's gradebook, so I said, 'I bet I can get a "B."' The less work God has to do to scale my grade up to that perfect score, the happier He's going to be with me. So God's Word was a tool for me.

Now, again, as I said earlier, the Bible certainly gives us instruction. It teaches us lessons that apply directly to our lives and current situations and circumstances and decisions. But if we only imagine the Bible as a teacher, we'll miss the beauty of it. When we first open the Bible, our temptation is to ask, 'God, what can I learn from this passage?' or 'God, how can I apply this passage to my life?' Those aren't bad questions, but they also shouldn't be the first questions we ask.

What if, instead, we prayed, 'God, how can I know you better through this passage?' I started asking that question a couple of years ago, and it changed the way I viewed the Scriptures. I actually began to see that God was my friend (John 15:5) and that He wanted me to know Him.

If we're just reading the Bible to get a high grade in God's book, we've completely missed the point. The Gospel tells us that we have all fallen short of God's glory, and we can only be saved by trusting in Christ's perfect 'score' of righteousness and trusting in His death, burial, and resurrection. We don't read the Bible to be a better Christian. We read the Bible to know Christ better.

IT'S A MARATHON, NOT A SPRINT

So, first piece of advice—ask the right question. Second piece of practical advice for reading the Bible—*it's a marathon, not a sprint.*

I'm not much of a long-distance runner. In all my years of athletic training, I could barely run more than a mile before I had to stop and take a long, LONG break. I was much better at running short distances as hard and fast as I could before I quickly reached the end of my fuse and fell to the ground in exhaustion. I was just never very good at pacing myself.

It wasn't until I was in my thirties that I realized I had been reading God's Word the same way for my entire life. Here's what I mean. January 1st rolled around every year with that mountain of a Bible reading plan standing before me, and I decided I would climb it by reading at least 10 chapters a day.

Day 1, I'm 100% bought in. I'm already at the Tower of Babel when I open my Bible on January 2nd, just absolutely crushing it! I keep sprinting through the Scriptures 10 chapters at a time for the first week or two until one day I look up and realize I'm getting burned out. I decide to take a break—a Sabbath if you will—and I remind myself that my Bible reading plan isn't about impressing God. Yeah, that sounds right. Two days later, I take another break. One week later, I'm reading less than three chapters a day, and by the time I get to Leviticus, I'm done, falling on the floor in exhaustion, tossing my Bible up on the nightstand to collect dust until December 31st.

I don't know if that sounds familiar to you, but I've repeated this pattern more times in my life than I'd wish to admit. When I finally came to the realization that reading my Bible was like running a marathon, everything suddenly seemed to click. I realized that I couldn't keep up the sprinting pace I had set for myself throughout an entire year. I also realized that reading the Scriptures was not just a year-long project. It's a lifelong journey that works much better with a slow and steady pace.

So I came up with an incredibly simple plan. I picked a book of the Bible I wanted to read through—Joshua—and I read one chapter a day. I didn't push myself to go further; I just lingered slowly on that one chapter, then closed my Bible and spent time in prayer. The next day I did the same thing. And again. And again, until several months later I found that I had slowly read a significant portion of Scripture. If I missed a day, I didn't try to make it up by reading two chapters the next day; I just picked up where I left off.

Over time, I began to see my hunger for God's Word grow. I woke up each morning with a real, genuine desire to open my Bible and spend time listening to the story of the Lord. Some days I read more than one chapter— several even—but I never did it out of some self-imposed regulation. I did it because I was beginning to love listening to God's story in a way that I never had before.

And there's nothing magical about the amount I had chosen to read each day. It's not like 'a chapter a day keeps the devil away' as I used to hear some people say growing up. I just found the right pace of Scripture reading that worked well for me. Some people might say I wasn't reading enough. Could I have read more and been more disciplined? Sure. But after a month of time, I had read over 31 chapters of the Bible. Ask yourself, when was the last time you read 31 chapters of God's Word in one month?

CONDITION YOUR HEART TO LISTEN

God's story is a marathon, and I believe it's helpful for us to pace ourselves and absorb it in small doses, especially when we first begin. We need to be conditioned to run this race, not just for a short period of time, but for the rest of our lives so that we might revisit this book again and again as we grow older and listen to the Word of Christ, walking with Him daily.

God has invited you to listen to His story because He wants you to know Him and trust Him. Read it slowly. Take your time. When you open your Bible, don't just ask God to help you learn things. Ask God to help you know Him, and then you will have learned the greatest thing of all—the face of the living God.

Main Point

Reading your Bible is like running a marathon, not a sprint.

Questions for Reflection

- What do you find to be the hardest part about reading your Bible?
- Have you ever thought it might not be your method of reading that's wrong but your view of Scripture as a whole? If the Bible is just a history book, it gets old after a while. But if we see it as a love letter to us, it becomes much more precious.
- What does it mean to you to say that reading your Bible is more like running a marathon instead of a sprint?

6. God's Story Is True

Growing up in the South, when someone wasn't telling the truth, we used to say they were telling a *story*. I'm not quite sure how the word 'story' became synonymous with 'false' or 'made up,' but because of that, I've always struggled to think of a story as anything other than a lie.

Isn't that exactly what so many people think of the Bible, especially when we call it a *story*? You may be asking yourself, 'What's the point of reading my Bible if I don't even know whether or not it's true?'

Well, that's a really important question because if the Bible's not true, there's no point in even opening it, let alone reading it. I'm not an apologist or a scholar, and I don't have the expertise to give a full-scale answer as to why you should trust the Bible. But I can give you a few helpful points and arguments that have

41

helped me trust God's Word in the past. The first point I want to look at is actually the main point of the story—Jesus Himself.

THE PERSON OF JESUS

There are numerous accounts of the life of Jesus outside of the Bible that were written even as early as the first century AD. Many of these writers and historical documents (Tacitus, Josephus, and the Babylonian Talmud, to name a few) do not claim that Jesus was God, however, they could not deny His existence.

Many of these Jewish historians went so far as to call Jesus a sorcerer who practiced magic and led Israel astray[1]. That's fascinating, isn't it? These documents were written by the blatant enemies of the early Christian church; if they were trying to disprove the Christian faith, would they not just say that the disciples were lying about Jesus' miracles? Why would they call Jesus a sorcerer?

Well, many of the people who witnessed those miracles were alive during the writings of these first century documents and could have very easily discredited the words of the historians had they denied the things the

---

1   Strobel, Lee, *The Case for Christ,* 1996.

people had seen with their own eyes. In other words, if the enemies of Jesus had to call Him a sorcerer to explain the things He had done, then it's likely that Jesus did supernatural things.

Speaking of eyewitnesses, Paul said in 1 Corinthians 15:6 that Jesus appeared to more than 500 people at once. Then he added the phrase, 'many of whom are still alive.' Why would Paul say that? If your grandmother was a living, breathing survivor of the Holocaust, and you heard someone at school try to spread a rumor that the Holocaust had never happened, what would you say? You'd say, 'My grandmother was there! And she's still alive! Go talk to her if you have doubts about that story.'

Paul does the same thing here. 1 Corinthians was written somewhere between 20 to 25 years after the death of Jesus, and Paul was inviting any doubters to go speak to the eyewitnesses of the Resurrection who were still alive so that they could tell their side of the story. If the Resurrection wasn't true, then why would Paul invite such open scrutiny of his story?

If the Resurrection is true, however, then we have to conclude that Jesus is exactly who He said He was—the Son of God Almighty, Creator of heaven and earth. And if Jesus is who He said He was, and Jesus believed the Scriptures (which He *did*—Matthew 5:17-18, Luke 24:44, John 17:17), then we can believe the Scriptures as well. The authenticity of the Bible hinges on our opinion of who Jesus was.

But there's a second point that I find fascinating, and it has to do with Jesus' disciples.

THE COURAGE OF THE DISCIPLES

On the night Jesus was arrested, His disciples were, quite frankly, scared to death (Mark 14:43-50). They all fled the scene when the authorities took Him away in chains. They were frightened and confused, and they thought they would have to die with Jesus if they were discovered to be His followers.

But then in Acts 4:5-13, we see a completely different spirit in them. Something had changed. Something had given them boldness to preach the Gospel and stand before the very same people who had crucified Jesus weeks earlier. Something had given them courage to call themselves the Apostles and the followers of Jesus Christ.

What happened? They had all personally encountered the Resurrected Christ, that's what happened. And they were never the same from that day forth. Instead of running away as they had in the Garden, they marched to the corners of the earth, preaching the Gospel to the nations, telling their story to brothers and sisters everywhere in what has now grown to be the largest religion in the world[2].

Here's an important question to consider: why would they do that if the Resurrection wasn't true? If Jesus never rose from the dead, it means the disciples weren't just mistaken; it means they were *lying*. They were the ones who claimed to have seen the risen Jesus, and they endured torture, pain, suffering, and death at the hands of people who did not wish for their story to be told.

I've heard it said that some people have died for believing in a lie, but no one in history has ever died for believing a lie of their own making. If the Resurrection isn't true, then why did every single one of the disciples throw their lives away for nothing more than a practical joke? The only conclusion I can come up with

---

2   McLaughlin,   Rebecca,   *Confronting   Christianity*
(2019), 12.

is that the stories are, in fact, true. It's the only explanation that makes sense to me. Which brings us to our last point.

THE BRILLIANCE OF THE STORY

I was an English major in college, and I spent a lot of time studying literary critique—how to judge what makes a story good or bad. The quality of a story has a lot to do with a device we call 'theme.'

A theme is an idea or topic that consistently occurs throughout a story. The more epic and grand and expansive the story is, the harder it becomes to maintain unity and consistency throughout the major themes.

In my limited expertise, I can say with absolute confidence that I have never read or seen or heard a story with a more brilliant and cohesive theme as the Bible. If the Bible had been written as a piece of fiction by one single author, it would undoubtedly be considered by scholars everywhere to be the greatest work of literature ever written. But it's not fiction. And it was written by several different authors spanning several centuries of time. The story is so masterful in its thematic arrangement that it's hard to believe so many different people had a hand in writing it down.

Yet, all of these authors who contributed had one thing in common—they all believed that there was another Author behind them telling a much bigger story—a story even they could not fully see at the time. This may sound childish or implausible, but I believe in the truth of the Scriptures because I'm convinced it's too good of a story to have been invented by man.

God saved those who took shelter from the flood inside the ark just as He saves those who take shelter beneath the cross of Jesus. God spared Abraham's son Isaac on the altar only to offer up His own Son as the ultimate sacrifice many centuries later. Samson spread his arms between the pillars and destroyed God's enemies, dying among them just as Jesus spread His arms on the cross and did the same. Boaz redeemed the foreign woman Ruth by making her his wife just as Christ redeemed His exiled, wandering people by making us His bride. David became champion of the Israelites by slaying the giant just as Jesus became the champion of God's family by defeating Death in the tomb. And Jesus crushed the head of the very serpent who had first deceived man and woman in the Garden just as God promised He would all the way back in Genesis 3.

Jesus is the fulfillment of all the stories and all the images and all the prophecies that were written about Him hundreds of years before He was even born. This story is just, to put it plainly, too perfect to be made up. The only way it makes sense is if it was written in supernatural ink by a supernatural Author. And this is exactly what 2 Peter 1:20-21 tells us: 'No prophecy of Scripture comes from someone's own interpretation. For no prophecy was ever produced by the will of man, but men spoke from God as they were carried along by the Holy Spirit.'

TOO GOOD NOT TO BE TRUE

The story of God's Word is too compelling to be brushed aside as fantastical or fiction. I believe it all hinges on Jesus and the Resurrection, and I have yet to find anything that has persuaded me to believe it's not true.

I have found plenty of stories in this world, on the other hand, that have led me to believe in the presence of another master storyteller who wishes to distract us from God's truth.

'Our enemy the devil prowls around like a roaring lion seeking to devour us' (1 Pet. 5:8) with the false narratives we consume every single day. If we don't pay attention to the stories he is telling us, then we'll find ourselves falling asleep in the poppy field just like Dorothy and her friends before we even know what hit us.

What are some of these stories? We'll tackle that in the next chapter.

Main Point

The Bible is true, not just because it says it is, but because historical evidence points us to that conclusion.

Questions for Reflection

- Have you ever doubted the Bible? What are the things that make you doubt it the most or find hardest to believe? (I'd encourage you to write those things down.)
- Were there any points brought up in this chapter that you had never thought about before?
- How should your view of Jesus affect the way you view the rest of Scripture?
- If you took the time to write down your doubts, I'd encourage you to pray about them or bring them to a trusted friend or

pastor and talk about them. God never intended us to just figure this stuff out on our own. He put characters (relationship) in your story to walk alongside you in this journey.

7. The False Narratives of the World

In 2009, two men named Joshua Glenn and Rob Walker designed a human experiment called 'Significant Objects' where they bought hundreds of worthless antique knick-knacks for a total of $128.74. Their goal was to resell the items on eBay by adding one thing only—a story. They hired over 100 creative writers to add completely fabricated interesting, funny or sentimental backstories under the description of every single object.

The result? People bought it hook, line, and sinker. Over the course of four months, every single object ended up selling for a total of... drum roll please...$3612.51! If you're doing the math, that's almost a 3000% return on investment from nothing more than made up stories.[1]

---

1   www.significantobjects.com

It's easy for us to criticize the online buyers for being gullible suckers and believing something so ridiculous, but let's stop and think for a moment about what happened.

Glenn and Walker's experimental hypothesis was this: 'Narrative transforms insignificant objects into significant ones.' And they were 100% correct. Stories shape us. Even the false ones. And Satan, our enemy, knows this as well as anyone.

In Genesis 3:4-5, we are introduced to the Devil as he pointed Eve to the forbidden fruit and said, 'You will not surely die. For God knows that when you eat of it your eyes will be opened, and you will be like God, knowing good and evil.' The first thing he ever said in the Garden was a false narrative meant to lead God's people astray.

Satan is constantly at work trying to deceive us, and many of those lies have taken root in the modern, secularized culture we live in. It's important for us, as followers of Christ, to be mindful of these stories whenever we hear them, so let's talk about a few of the ones that are so prevalent today.

LISTEN TO YOUR HEART

One of my favorite movies growing up was *The Sandlot*. It is a coming-of-age tale set in the 1950s about a group of young boys who played baseball together every day.

One day they accidentally hit a Babe Ruth autographed ball over the fence into a neighbor's yard, and in this yard lived a giant dog they called 'The Beast.' The kids struggled every which way they could to get the ball back without being eaten.

One night, Benny, the hero of the story, had a dream where he was visited by the ghost of Babe Ruth. The Babe's advice: 'follow your heart, kid, and you'll never go wrong.'

That stuck with me for a long time to the point where I thought the key to making good decisions in life was listening to my heart. As I grew older, I soon came to realize that Babe Ruth wasn't the only one handing out that piece of advice.

In Disney's 2013 *Frozen*, the protagonist Elsa sings, 'Let it go, let it go, can't hold it back anymore' as she regretfully realizes she spent her whole life silencing her inner voice. In Disney's 2016 *Moana*, the grandmother sings the breakthrough song, 'When that voice starts to whisper, "follow the farthest star," Moana, that voice inside is who you are.' And all the way back in 1988, Roxette sang her hit single 'Listen to Your Heart.'

This story is everywhere, and here's what it's actually saying: 'Don't let anybody tell you who you can or can't be. You can do anything you want. Believe in yourself. Listen to your heart, and you'll be just fine.' Does some variation of that sound familiar to you? I'm sure if you think about it, you'll realize you've been hearing that advice your whole life, and it's especially loud in the 21st century.

What does the Bible have to say about listening to our hearts? Let's start with Jeremiah 17:9: 'The heart is deceitful above all things and desperately sick; who can understand it?' Jeremiah doesn't mince words. He flat out tells us that our hearts are corrupted with sin and should not be trusted.

If we can't trust our hearts, then where do we turn? Proverbs 3:5 says, 'Trust in the Lord with all your heart, and do not lean on your own understanding.' Scripture tells us that we have to trust and listen to words that come from outside of ourselves—the Word of the Lord. Interestingly enough, the Word of God was the first thing Satan attacked in the Garden—in Genesis 3:1, he began by asking Eve, 'Did God actually say…?'

See how he weaves together that story of doubt. Satan doesn't want us looking to God's Word for guidance; he wants us looking to our own understanding while we question the words of the Lord. He wants us to listen to our own hearts. But as we have seen from Scripture, Satan is lying to us, and he only means us harm.

YOU ARE YOUR OWN HERO

If you google the phrase 'be your own hero,' you'll find pages and pages of positive, uplifting, and motivational articles, blogs and images championing this mantra of self-reliance. The idea is this: 'Life is hard, the world's got you down, but you don't need somebody else to come in and rescue you from your problems. All you need to do is think positive thoughts, don't give up, and be your own hero.'

On the surface, this may not sound like a bad message, especially when seen through the lens of the modern, Western, enlightened individual who's been taught their whole lives 'you can do anything you set your mind to.' The world loves stories where ordinary people decide to be strong and brave and pick themselves up by the bootstraps in an act of self-liberation. At least, that's what the world thinks it wants.

But what are the kind of stories we actually crave? How about the most popular movie franchise in history which, at the time of this writing, owns five of the top ten box office spots of *all time*? I'm talking about the Marvel Cinematic Universe. And what is this franchise all about? It's about a world full of people who can't save themselves from their greatest problems, so they turn to a band of heroes who, at great cost to themselves, step in to save the day.

If the world really wants to see stories that encourage us to be our own heroes, then why does the image of Thor smashing onto the battlefield when all hope is lost make grown men and women go absolutely nuts in the theaters? Because ultimately, in the depths of our hearts, we know we're not Thor. We know that we're actually the ones getting overrun by the enemy, and deep down in places we don't like to talk about, we're just hoping to God that there's a hero out there who's bigger than us, who loves us, and who's willing to risk everything to save us.

Telling someone they should save themselves is not good news. It's actually the worst news on the planet. It's despairing and hopeless, and that's not the news God left for His people in the Old Testament. When they were slaves in Egypt, they weren't told to keep their chin up and think positive thoughts. They were told about a deliverer—a messiah—who would set them free from tyranny, and his name was Moses.

When God's people were slaves to sin (Isa. 9) and walking in darkness, they believed they would one day see a glorious light. They weren't told, however, that the light was inside them all along. They were told that the light would come to them from above. The light would shine on them, and that light would be the Light of the world. And to them a child was born. To them a son was given, and His name was Wonderful Counselor, Mighty God, Everlasting Father, Prince of Peace (Isa. 9:6). His name was Jesus, the one, true Messiah.

Satan wants us to believe that we don't need a hero. Satan wants us to believe that the best thing we could ever do is to find the hero within. Because if we've found a hero within us, why would we ever need Jesus?

NO REST FOR THE WEARY

If you're tired, you're doing something right. That's what the world wants you to think. If you're busy and weary and at the end of your rope, it means you're on the path to success. And if you're not exhausted or anxious or stressed every night when you go to sleep, you must not be working hard enough. You're going to fall behind your peers, and they're going to get that college admission/scholarship/social standing/reputation/job/relationship that you so desperately desire.

In other words, you can rest when you retire, and the harder you work now, the earlier you'll be able to retire. Isn't that the goal of life? Work as hard as you can now without stopping to get enough money and power and success to make you and your family comfortable so that the last couple of decades of your life can be spent in leisure.

Satan loves that story. It's one of his favorites, and he's gotten most people to spend their very souls in effort to buy it. What does the Bible say about this story?

In Exodus 20, the Lord gave the Ten Commandments to the Israelites just as they had left their lives of slavery in Egypt. The fifth commandment in verses 9-10 says, 'Six days you shall labor, and do all your work, but the seventh day is a Sabbath to the Lord your God. On it you shall not do any work.'

It's been said that the commandments of God are also the graces of God because He made us—He knows exactly what boundaries we need in order to flourish and thrive in His creation. In this beautiful commandment, we see the Lord guiding His children into the sweetness of His rest, essentially saying, 'You were once slaves in Egypt, but now you are free. I will not have you becoming slaves to your own labor. I will teach you to rest in Me and to trust in My work.'

Now, this is not to say we shouldn't work hard at what the Lord has put in front of us. God is glorified when we pursue our work with excellence. But He is also glorified when we put our work down in a weekly rhythm of Sabbath rest.

Here's the hard part—do you know what happens when you rest? You lose the rat race. If you take a break every week, you're going to fall behind the pack. You won't accomplish as much as your peers because you'll be choosing to lay aside your work once every seven days. But you'll also find yourself growing healthier in both body and soul. You'll learn to trust Jesus more, and ultimately, you'll learn to taste the sweetness of the eternal rest He has secured for you in the New Heavens and New Earth.

DRAW NEAR TO THE LORD

In James 4:7 we read, 'Resist the devil, and he will flee from you.' If we were to say the opposite of that, it might sound something like, 'Draw near to the devil, and he will sing you to sleep with his stories.' It's easy to think about Satan as a big, bad monster with horns and a pitchfork. We don't often think of him as a beautiful, compelling narrator. It's become quite easy in this world to draw near to him and give him our ears.

So we must heed the very next verse in James 4:8: 'Draw near to God, and he will draw near to you.' He is the way, the truth, and the life, and He is the One who truly knows what is best for His people and for His creation. If we study His Word and meet regularly with other Christians then we will start to see that Satan's lies ring hollow, and we will grow better at recognizing them for what they truly are.

And as the Lord begins to uproot the false narratives in the soil around us, we'll begin to see more clearly the difference between a good story and a bad one—or perhaps another way of saying it, as we'll see in the next chapter, would be, the difference between a redemptive story and a destructive one.

Main Point

Satan tells stories that are close enough to the truth to make us believe them but far enough from the truth to deceive us.

Questions for Reflection

- Do you recognize any of these stories from Satan in other stories that you have heard in the world around you?
- What are some other false narratives you might have noticed in the stories you've heard or seen in the world?
- How do we discern the difference between the false narratives and the true, God-glorifying truths?

8. What Makes a Story Good?

In 1998, a small movie-review website called 'Rotten Tomatoes' was started by three students from the University of California, Berkeley. The purpose of the website was to provide simple, large-scale reviews of movies so that the public might better know what to expect when they walked into the theaters. It was patterned after the idea of people throwing rotten tomatoes onto a stage in the old days when they didn't like a performance.

'Rotten Tomatoes' has grown to be one of the most popular movie critic sites in the world right now because of its simplistic format. Instead of a reviewer rating a movie on a scale of 1–5, they give it either a simple thumbs up or thumbs down—a rotten tomato or a good one. The website then takes hundreds of different people's scores and averages them together on their 'Tomato-meter' for the final rating of the movie. The higher the score, the better the movie, the lower the score, the worse the movie—at least that's the theory behind it.

The problem with this format is that it assumes consensus equals quality. In other words, 'if all these people like it, it must be good.' While this design might be helpful for weeding out the bad movies, it still brings up essential questions like, *what makes a story good? Why do these critics hold so much weight in their opinion of good and bad? Is there such a thing as objective goodness or beauty? And how do we, as Christians, learn how to determine the goodness or worth of a story?* Well, for that, we must look again to God's Word.

GOD'S STANDARD OF BEAUTY

In Paul's epistle to the church in Philippi we read, 'Finally, brothers, whatever is true, whatever is honorable, whatever is just, whatever is pure, whatever is lovely, whatever is commendable, if there is any excellence, if there is anything worthy of praise, think about these things' (Phil. 4:8).

I once heard a pastor named Skip Ryan say, 'Beauty is not merely in the eyes of the beholder. There is a standard of beauty in this world because there is a beautiful One.'[1] The way we judge the quality of a story is by comparing its beauty and goodness to that of the Lord's. In this verse in Philippians, Paul gave us the template for God's idea of objective beauty. Now, we also know that every story is eventually going to fall short of that standard, right? No story compares to the Bible in its portrayal of the Lord's beauty.

Are we supposed to just ignore any story but the Bible, then? No, because if the Bible is the story that drives our hearts, then we can rely on God-given wisdom to discern the goodness and beauty of all the other stories we consume throughout our daily lives. And discernment begins by asking the right questions.

BIBLICAL QUESTIONS TO ASK OURSELVES

'Is this story *true?*' This is the first word Paul uses in Philippians 4:8. It doesn't mean that a story has to be nonfiction or historical. It means that it needs to convey the universal truth of God's established order. Sin and idolatry lead to brokenness; selflessness and sacrifice lead to

---

1   Quoted from a seminary class on 'Spiritual Theology' I took from Rev. Skip Ryan at Redeemer Seminary in Houston, TX in fall of 2011.

life. A good story will tell the *truth* about these qualities.

'Is this story honorable/commendable/worthy of praise?' For the sake of time and space, I'll lump these descriptions into the same category because they all make a similar point—God wants us to dwell on things we would want to share with the world. The stories we consume in the dark, in our rooms, by ourselves—the stories most of us wouldn't want our parents to know about—those stories aren't commendable or worthy of praise. Paul is calling the Christian to think about the sort of things and engage in the sort of stories we would want to share and lift up to the people around us.

'Is this story pure/lovely/just?' Another way of saying it would be, 'Is this story redemptive?' Redemptive actually means more than just having a happy ending. A redemptive story doesn't have an absence of darkness, rather, it sheds light on the darkness and shows true immorality for the destructive monster that it really is. It also shows love and charity and self-sacrifice for the light-giving hero that it is. That's what makes the story pure and just and moral.

And when we talk about the word 'lovely,' we could say that content matters as well. The Bible is full of some really gritty content, but it also doesn't glorify that content. A lovely story is one that, while showing us the truth, refrains from being grotesque or overly indulgent in its graphic depictions of sin and darkness. It remains honest and tasteful while pointing us to the light.

HOW TO DISCERN EXCELLENCE

Lastly, 'Is this story excellent?' That's a fairly all-encompassing question, and it requires a good deal of discernment involving other smaller questions. Does the story do a good job of *showing* rather than *telling*? Does the story have well-crafted characters with believable and relatable motivations? Does the story have traces of love from its creator, or does it feel like it was rushed or made simply for money or mass appeal?

And the mark of excellence is not black and white. It's not as if a story goes from being bad to good when it reaches a certain score on the 'excellence-meter.' There's a scale, and some stories are filled with more excellence than others.

Most stories have both good *and* bad in them because, as I said before, there's only one perfect story. However, the more a story is created with love and skill and determination, the more its excellence will shine. These are the stories I believe are pleasing to the Lord and should, in turn, be pleasing to us as we grow in faith and begin to pattern our tastes after God's own.

You want a really nerdy example of this? Watch the behind the scenes footage of *The Lord of the Rings* movie trilogy, and then watch those from *The Hobbit*. The first franchise was very clearly created with excellence at every corner, on every set, in every wardrobe, on every script, in every frame.

The second franchise wasn't bad, but it felt more rushed and overextended. It felt like a story that was being told more for the sake of money and mass appeal than for the sake of love. That's just my opinion, but you'd be hard pressed to find anyone who doesn't agree that *The Lord of the Rings* movies are more excellent than *The Hobbit*.

A LIGHT IN THE DARK

I know this is a lot to think about when we examine the goodness or badness of a story, and it's rarely as simple as just calling it 'good' or 'bad.' There is such a thing as *subjective* beauty, too. We don't have to enjoy everything equally, and we don't have to enjoy everything that is *objectively* good. God has given us all individual tastes and preferences, but as we grow in Christ, it's important to make sure that we are developing a taste for things that lead to life, not destruction. You don't have to like broccoli just because it's good for you. But don't let Oreos be the replacement for broccoli in your diet. Find another *objectively* healthy food that appeals to your *subjective* tastes. (But if the Oreos are double stuffed…sure, go right ahead).

In all seriousness, here's another way to think of it—the more dimly lit a room is, the harder it is to see. So if we imagine the qualities of Philippians 4:8 as lamps in a room, then we can know that a good story is going to be well lit because it will be shining with truth and love and purity and honor and excellence. It will be a story that lights our way and helps us see the truth of who we really are and what we were made for.

On that note, let me give you a word of warning—the more time you spend enjoying bad or 'dimly lit' stories (whether that be certain movies, books, music, video games or even social media accounts), the more your eyes will begin to adjust to the darkness. God has not called us to be spiritually nocturnal. We are creatures of the day, called to live in the light. Ephesians 5:8-9 reads, 'For at one time you were darkness, but now you are light in the Lord. Walk as children of light (for the fruit of light is found in all that is good and right and true).'

Determining the objective beauty of a story may not always be as simple as labeling it *good* or *bad*. But the more we frame our hearts with the beauty of God's story, the more we will be able to tell the difference between the stories that carry that same torch and the ones that lead us into the shadows.

Main Point

God's standard of beauty is what helps us judge the goodness or worth of a story.

Questions for Reflection

- Have you ever thought about the difference between objective beauty (something that is universally good by God's standards) and subjective beauty (something that appeals to your specific tastes)?

- How do we develop our subjective tastes to line up with God's objective qualities of goodness?
- Why is it so dangerous for us to continually indulge ourselves with stories that lead us into darkness away from God's purity?

9. Your Story Has an Author

Near the turn of the century in London, England, there lived an author by the name of Sir Arthur Conan Doyle. He was an aspiring writer of historical fiction with the desire to be as famous and well-known as English authors the likes of Charles Dickens. However, he could find no one to publish his works.

One day, an upstart magazine called *The Strand* approached Doyle about writing a series of short stories in the 'detective' genre. Against his better wishes, Doyle agreed because he was in desperate need of money to pay the rent.

In 1887, *Strand Magazine* published 'A Study in Scarlet' debuting what is widely considered to be one of the all-time greatest characters in the history of Western literature—*Sherlock Holmes*. Fans around London went wild, and

The Strand's subscriptions went through the roof. Doyle became an overnight success.

However, little known to most people, Doyle actually despised the detective genre. For starters, if you're going to write about Sherlock Holmes, you have to be smarter than Sherlock Holmes. Not an easy task. Second, the constant plotting and maneuvering involved in writing mysteries of that sort was mentally draining, leaving him little time and energy to write about the things he loved. Doyle wrote a letter to his mother in 1891 saying, 'I think of slaying Holmes…and winding him up for good and all. He takes my mind from better things.' [1]

So in his 1893 short story *The Final Problem*, Doyle killed his main character and put an end to it.

When London read it, they went into an uproar, and *Strand Magazine* panicked. They begged him to continue writing, so Doyle raised his price to an absurd amount, thinking they would never meet it. Well, they did. And Doyle became one of the wealthiest authors in the world and reluctantly continued writing

---

1   Carr, John Dickson, *The Life of Sir Arthur Conan Doyle* (1949), 66.

about the cunning sleuth for the rest of his days.

Near the end of his life, Doyle admitted regret over his beloved creation. He was quoted as saying, 'I believe if I had never touched Holmes...my position in literature would at the present moment be a more commanding one.'[2]

I don't know why, but that makes me sad. It's not that I care that much about Sherlock Holmes. It makes me sad, however, to hear an author talk about his main character that way because, deep down inside, if I'm being completely honest, sometimes I can't help but wonder if my Author feels the same way about me.

I'm not easy to love. I'm a stubborn, prideful, self-centered, wandering soul. I often make the same mistakes over and again. I've broken vows with my Maker I never thought I'd break. And worst of all, I can't think of one single night in my life when my head has hit the pillow with the confidence that I had loved Jesus with my whole heart, soul, and mind that day. Bottom line, I have not lived up to who He made me to be.

---

2   Miller, John J. 'The Burden of Holmes' from *The Wall Street Journal*, Dec. 23, 2009.

DOES OUR AUTHOR LOVE US?

So how do we know our Author doesn't feel the same way about us as Sir Arthur Conan Doyle felt about his creation? Well, perhaps we can take a glance at one of my favorite stories of all time—*The Lord of the Rings*.

It was a major motion picture trilogy that won 11 Oscars and captivated the world with a deep dive into the fantasy land of J.R.R. Tolkien's Middle Earth. However, as good as the movies were, there was one scene from the books that director Peter Jackson conveniently left out of *The Fellowship of the Ring*.

In this scene, Frodo and his friends are on their quest to destroy the One Ring of Power when they come across an old hermit in the woods named Tom Bombadil. Tom is a jolly recluse who lives in a cabin, tends to the plants and animals and sings nonsense songs all day long. He's married to a river goddess and claims he's older than the trees. In other words, he's kind of eccentric.

Tom invites the hobbits into his home for dinner, and when he hears of Frodo's quest to destroy the Ring, Tom asks if he can hold it. Frodo is suspicious because Gandalf, the great wizard, couldn't even look at the ring without being tempted by it, but he eventually agrees. Tom takes the Ring and flicks it up in the air, and suddenly, without warning, it vanishes. Then he reaches around and pulls it out from behind his back, grinning from ear to ear.

Tom Bombadil was doing magic tricks with the Ring of Power like he was at a five-year-old's birthday party!

Next, he slips the Ring on his own finger and *doesn't* disappear like everyone else. Needless to say, Frodo's mind is boggled at this point, and he begins to think that maybe Tom has pulled a fast one on him. He thinks Tom must have switched the Ring when it was behind him, so Frodo sneaks into the corner of the house while no one is watching and puts the Ring on his own finger. Sure enough, he disappears, and Frodo realizes that it is still the true Ring of Power.

Frodo sits there invisible, astounded, trying to make sense of how Tom had managed to avert the power of the One Ring when suddenly, Tom looks over in his direction. Through the haze of invisibility, Tom whispers, 'I see you over there, Frodo. Why don't you take off that ring and come join us?'[3]

---

3   J.R.R. Tolkien, *The Fellowship of the Ring*, chapter 7.

Tom saw Frodo when no one else could! And after that chapter in the book, Tom is barely mentioned throughout the rest of the entire story. He didn't progress the plot forward at all. He was little more than a way station on Frodo's journey. So why was he in the story? Was Tom the most powerful character in Middle Earth? If so, why didn't he do more? Scholars and critics alike asked all these questions and more when the books came out, but Tolkien remained mysteriously silent on the topic of Tom Bombadil.

Throughout the years, scholars composed an interesting theory regarding Tom, and although Tolkien never confirmed it, he also never denied it. The theory is this—Tom Bombadil was actually J.R.R. Tolkien *himself*. In other words, Tolkien loved Middle Earth, his own creation, so much that he wrote himself into the story at one of the most pivotal parts of the journey for Frodo and his friends.

Now, I don't know if that's actually true, but if it is, I think I know where Tolkien got the idea. You see, Tolkien was a Christian. And there's another story where the Author does just that. It's the greatest story ever told—the story of the Almighty God, the Author of all creation who, long ago, made all things good. But when His creation ruined all that He had made, a curse fell upon the land like a shadow. Hero after hero rose and fell, unable to save God's people completely. So on an ordinary night, in an ordinary town called Bethlehem, in the presence of ordinary shepherds and livestock, a baby cried, and that baby was the Way, the Truth, and the Life. The Author Himself entered into His own story, not merely to guide or teach His children, but to save them when they could not save themselves.

Your story has an Author, and your Author loves you (Heb. 12:1-2). And if you have believed in Him and placed your trust in His righteousness and not your own, then your story is not just written in love; it's written in blood. His blood. The Author lived, died, and rose again so that our story might be redeemed. And we look forward to the fullness of that redemption when we get to see our Author face to face.

Main Point

Your story has an Author, and He loves you very much.

Questions for Reflection

- Is it strange for you to think of yourself as a character in a story?
- Does it help to think of yourself as a character if you have a better understanding of your Author's motivations?
- Do you ever think that your Author, your Creator, looks at you as if you are a waste of space?
- God, our Author, wrote Himself into His own story in order to redeem His people. How does that change the way you view your Author?

10. Your Story Has an Ending

In 2017, Disney released a live-action remake of their classic animated hit *Beauty and the Beast*. It was essentially the same story, good but slightly sub-par compared to the original. There was one small difference in the remake, however, that I believe raised the stakes a notch or two.

For those of you unfamiliar with the story, it's a classic fairy tale about a mean, spoiled prince who gets cursed by a witch and turned into a Beast. The curse, however, extends beyond the prince, falling over everything and everyone in the castle, basically turning them into talking pieces of furniture until the Beast is able to find love.

In the original animated version, the Beast has to find love before the last petal falls from his flower or else they all stay in their current condition under the curse. In the newer, live-action version, if the Beast does not find love, everyone dies, losing what little they had left of their humanity as they turn into still, cold, silent pieces of décor.

As I said, the stakes are higher.

At the end of the great battle, there is a gut-wrenching scene where the Beast dies, the last petal falls, and everyone in the castle feels death descending on them like fog in the night. Old friends, families and loved ones utter desperate goodbyes, believing they will never see each other again. They break off mid-sentence becoming cold and lifeless as the curse presses its full weight down on the castle, choking the very life out of it.

It's a devastating moment to witness on screen, but even in that moment, most of the people watching knew that the hero was on her way. Sure enough, Belle rides in, kneels down, gives her heart to the Beast, whispers, 'I love you,' and the spell is broken. The curse is lifted, and death is reversed.

Now, here's the part I don't want you to miss—when the curse was lifted, the dead servants didn't just go back to being talking pieces of furniture. Oh, no. That would have been a disappointing ending, to say the least. In this story, when the curse was lifted, every corner of the castle, every servant in the home, even the Beast himself was restored to the fullest version of themselves, the people and the home they were meant to be all along.

That's the New Heavens and the New Earth. That's the Resurrection that Jesus has promised for His people and for His creation. That's how the story will end for those who believe in Christ.

THE BIBLE'S PICTURE OF ETERNITY

And I heard a loud voice from the throne saying, 'Behold, the dwelling place of God is with man. He will dwell with them, and they will be his people, and God himself will be with them as their God. He will wipe away every tear from their eyes, and death shall be no more, neither shall there be mourning, nor crying, nor pain anymore, for the former things have passed away.' And he who was seated on the throne said, 'Behold, I am making all things new' (Rev. 21:3-5).

This is the picture of eternity that the Apostle John paints for us in the last book of the Bible after

83

Christ has come back a second time to destroy the curse and all His enemies once and for all. I've heard this pointed out by many pastors and theologians who are much smarter than I am—God never said, 'I am making all new things.' He said, 'I am making all *things new*.'

We don't get a brand-new creation when Jesus comes back. We get the same creation that we know and love filled with trees and mountains and rivers and homes and loved ones and art and food and friendship, except that all of these things—the good things that are preserved after the curse has been melted away—they will all be *made new* for our pleasure and for the Lord's glory (Rom. 8:18-23, 2 Pet. 3:10-13).

THE DWELLING OF GOD IS WITH MAN

Also, notice the refrain that is repeated here for the last time throughout Scripture—'Behold the dwelling of God is with man.' *With* man. That's always been God's mission. When God put Adam and Eve in the Garden, He walked among them and made His home in the place that they called home.

When the Israelites wandered through the wilderness, God pitched His tent among theirs and called it the Tabernacle, making His home in the place that they called home. When His people were lost in the darkness of their sin, He entered into that darkness, becoming flesh and dwelling among them, making His home in the place that they called home.

Eternity is no different. God does not plan on blowing up the earth and bringing us to some alien planet where we live in the clouds with Him forever and play harps in a world where every good thing we ever loved is gone. In Revelation, we see an image of God Almighty coming down to earth again and making His dwelling *with* us! He makes His home in the place that we call home, and He remakes it the way it was always meant to be.

And He remakes us into the people we were always meant to be, which means no more sin. No more insecurity. No more fear. No more addiction. No more violence. No more abandoned children. No more failed marriages. No more lonely nights. No more idolatry. No more suffering. No more tears. No more pain. The former things will pass away.

We will be made new, and we will worship God and love Him with all our hearts. And nothing else will ever compete for that love. It will be the greatest thing we will have ever experienced, and it will never end. We will feel more at home in the New Heavens and New Earth than we have ever felt in this life because it will be the home we were always made for.

THE END OF THE BEGINNING

Your life is a story, and if you are in Christ then God has prepared a grand finale to your story that is beyond your wildest imaginations.

I think C.S. Lewis said it best at the closing of *The Chronicles of Narnia: The Last Battle*. The Old Narnia had just been remade into the new one, and Lewis finished his epic children's fantasy series with these words: 'All their life in this world and all their adventures in Narnia had only been the cover and the title page: now at last they were beginning Chapter One of the Great Story which no one on earth has read: which goes on forever: in which every chapter is better than the one before.'[1]

When a story approaches its climax, we say it's 'the beginning of the end.' But our lives here on earth are just the cover and the title page of the story God is writing for us. So perhaps, as we think about the culmination of our days, we would be wise to call it 'the end

---

1   Lewis, C.S., *The Chronicles of Narnia: The Last Battle* (1956), 228.

of the beginning,' for our Lord and Savior has promised us so much more to look forward to at the turning of this page.

Main Point

The end of our story is the beginning of the life and the home we were always meant to have with our God.

Questions for Reflection

- What do you think about when you think of heaven? Is it scary? Is it happy? Is it boring?
- Was there anything in this chapter that maybe changed your expectations of eternity?
- Why is it so significant that God says, 'The dwelling of God is *with* man'?
- If heaven is the home we were always made for, then how might that change the way we live? How would it change the way we view our homes and possessions here in this life? How would it change the way we talk to people and interact with our classmates and love our neighbors? How does eternity and the resurrection change who we are right now?

Appendix A: What Now?

- Write down your five favorite movies and compare them to the qualities Paul mentions in Philippians 4:8. Is the story in each movie true, honorable, worthy of praise, excellent, etc.? Find other stories you enjoy—music, shows, books, etc.—continue this practice of submitting your thoughts to the Lord and asking Him to help guide you in wisdom as you think about the stories you love.
- Write down two or three questions you have that make it hard for you to believe the Bible. Take those questions to your parent or pastor or youth pastor and discuss them and pray about them asking that the Lord might open your eyes and give you faith.
- Pick a book of the Bible and read one chapter of it every day. And when you begin, pray that God would help you to

know Him better through that passage. Remember that what you are reading is God telling you His story so that you might know and trust Him more.

Appendix B: Other Books on this Topic

G.K. Chesterton, *Orthodoxy* (1908) (specifically the chapter 'The Ethics of Elfland').

Gordon D. Fee and Douglas Stuart, *How to Read the Bible Book by Book: A Guided Tour* (2012).

C.S. Lewis, *The Chronicles of Narnia* (1950–1956).

Sally Lloyd-Jones, *The Story of God's Love for You* (2015).

John Perritt, *Bible 101*, from Reformed Youth Ministry Resources.

Tony Reinke, *Lit! A Christian Guide to Reading Books* (2011).

Lee Strobel, *The Case for Christ: A Journalist's Personal Investigation of the Evidence for Jesus* (1996).

J.R.R. Tolkien, *The Lord of the Rings* (1954).

LIGON DUNCAN
& JOHN PERRITT

A Student's Guide to Sanctification

LIGON DUNCAN & JOHN PERRITT

Knowing that we have been saved by what Jesus has done rather than by what we have done is amazing. But how does this knowledge affect the way we live? What's the point in being good if we will be forgiven anyway? Actually the Bible says that God's forgiveness frees us to live for Him and through the Holy Spirit we can grow to become more and more like Jesus. Ligon Duncan and John Perritt dive into what that means in this short book.

978-1-5271-0451-8

EDWARD T.
WELCH

A Student's Guide to Anxiety

Edward T. Welch

We all know the feeling. That nervous, jittery, tense feeling that tells you that something bad is just ahead. Anxiety can be overwhelming. But the Bible has plenty to say to people who are anxious. This book will help us to take our eyes off our circumstances and fix them on God.

978-1-5271-0450-1

Reformed Youth Ministries (RYM) exists to reach students for Christ and equip them to serve. Passing the faith on to the next generation has been RYM's passion since it began. In 1972 three youth workers who shared a passion for biblical teaching to youth surveyed the landscape of youth ministry conferences. What they found was an emphasis on fun and games, not God's Word. Therefore, they started a conference that focused on the preaching and teaching of God's Word. Over the years RYM has grown beyond conferences into three areas of ministry: conferences, training, and resources.

- **Conferences:** RYM's youth conferences take place in the summer at a variety of locations across the United States and are continuing to expand. We also host parenting conferences throughout the year at local churches.

- **Training:** RYM launched an annual Youth Leader Training (YLT) conference in 2008. YLT has grown steadily through the years and is offered in multiple locations. RYM also offers a Church Internship Program in partnering local churches as well as youth leader coaching and youth ministry consulting.
- **Resources:** RYM offers a variety of resources for leaders, parents, and students. Several Bible studies are offered as free downloads with more titles regularly being added to their catalogue. RYM hosts multiple podcasts: *Parenting Today*, *The Local Youth Worker*, and *The RYM Student Podcast*, all of which can be downloaded on multiple formats. There are many additional ministry tools available for download on the website.

If you are passionate for passing the faith on to the next generation, please visit www.rym.org to learn more about Reformed Youth Ministries. If you are interested in partnering with us in ministry, please visit www.rym.org/donate.

Christian Focus Publications

Our mission statement —

STAYING FAITHFUL

In dependence upon God we seek to impact the world through literature faithful to His infallible Word, the Bible. Our aim is to ensure that the Lord Jesus Christ is presented as the only hope to obtain forgiveness of sin, live a useful life and look forward to heaven with Him.

Our books are published in four imprints:

CHRISTIAN
FOCUS

Popular works including biographies, commentaries, basic doctrine and Christian living.

CHRISTIAN
HERITAGE

Books representing some of the best material from the rich heritage of the church.

MENTOR

Books written at a level suitable for Bible College and seminary students, pastors, and other serious readers. The imprint includes commentaries, doctrinal studies, examination of current issues and church history.

CF4•K

Children's books for quality Bible teaching and for all age groups: Sunday school curriculum, puzzle and activity books; personal and family devotional titles, biographies and inspirational stories — because you are never too young to know Jesus!

Christian Focus Publications Ltd,
Geanies House, Fearn, Ross-shire,
IV20 1TW, Scotland, United Kingdom.
www.christianfocus.com
blog.christianfocus.com